MAKE IN A WEEKEND

POTHOLDERS & DISHCLOTHS

Want to spice up the kitchen for yourself or one of your favorite friends or relatives, but don't have a lot of time? Then get out your knitting needles and join us as we make it possible with these quick-to-knit potholders and dishcloths.

LEISURE ARTS, INC.
Maumelle, Arkansas

TOMATO POTHOLDER

Finished Size: 9½" diameter (24.13 cm)

EASY

Designed by Patricia Honaker

Cooking up a tomato dish? Add a tomato potholder when you deliver the dish to the dinner table.

SHOPPING LIST

Yarn

Medium-weight Cotton 4
[2.5 ounces, 120 yards
(70.9 grams, 109 meters) per ball]
red – 1 ball
green – 1 ball

Knitting Needles

24" (60.96 cm) size 7 (4.5 mm) circular needle (or size required for gauge)
Size 7 (4.5 mm) double-point needles (DPN) (or size required for gauge)

Additional Supplies

Stitch markers
Large-eye yarn needle

GAUGE INFORMATION

8 sts = 2" (5.08 cm)

STITCH GUIDE

Kfb: Knit 1 in front and back of same stitch.

SSK (slip, slip, knit): Slip 2 sts as to knit, one at a time to right-hand needle. Insert tip of left-hand needle into fronts of these slipped sts from left to right. Knit them together: one stitch has been decreased.

Note: *Except for the introduction in Rows 1-5, the entire pot holder is worked in rounds (Rnd). Begin the project with the double-point needles and switch to the circular needle when the number of stitches increases.*

Instructions continued on page 4

INSTRUCTIONS

Tomato (Make 2)

With red and DPN, CO 1 st.

Row 1: (K1, P1, K1) in same st: 3 sts.

Row 2: Purl across.

Row 3: Kfb all sts: 6 sts.

Row 4: Purl across.

Row 5: Repeat Row 3: 12 sts.

Rnd 1: Divide stitches onto 3 DPN (4 sts on each needle). Knit all sts, joining the round. Place marker on first stitch of round.

Rnd 2: *Kfb, K1; rep from * around: 18 sts.

Rnd 3: Knit around.

Rnd 4: Repeat Rnd 2: 27 sts.

Rnd 5: Knit around.

Rnd 6: *Kfb, K2; rep from * around: 36 sts.

Rnd 7: Purl around.

Rnd 8: *Kfb, K3; rep from * around: 45 sts.

Rnd 9: Knit around.

Rnd 10: *Kfb, K4; rep from * around: 54 sts.

Rnd 11: Knit around.

Rnd 12: *Kfb, K5 rep from * around: 63 sts.

Rnd 13: Knit around.

Rnd 14: *Kfb, K6; rep from * around: 72 sts.

Rnd 15: Purl around.

Rnd 16: *Kfb, K7; rep from * around: 81 sts.

Rnd 17: Knit around.

Rnd 18: *Kfb, K8; rep from * around: 90 sts.

Rnd 19: Knit around.

Rnd 20: *Kfb, K9; rep from * around: 99 sts.

Rnd 21: Purl around.

Rnd 22: *Kfb, K10; rep from * around: 108 sts.

Rnd 23: Knit around.

Rnd 24: *Kfb, K11; rep from * around: 117 sts.

Rnd 25: Purl around.

Rnd 26: *Kfb, K12; rep from * around: 126 sts.

Rnd 27: Purl around.

Rnd 28: *Kfb, K13; rep from * around: 135 sts.

Rnd 29: Purl around.

Rnd 30: SSK, K13, (Kfb, K14) 3 times, K15, (Kfb, K14) 3 times, Kfb, K12, K2tog, turn: 140 sts.

Rnd 31: SSK, knit to last 2 sts, K2tog, turn; 138 sts.

Rnd 32: SSK, K11, (Kfb, K15) 3 times, K15, (Kfb, K15) 3 times, Kfb, K11, K2tog, turn:143 sts.

Rnd 33: SSK, knit to last 2 sts, K2tog; 141 sts.

Bind off.

Leaves (Make 5)

With green and DPN, CO 6 sts.

Row 1: Sl st, K to end.

Row 2: Sl st, P to end.

Rows 3 – 12: Rep Rows 1 and 2.

Row 13: SSK, K2, K2tog.

Row 14: Sl st, P to end.

Row 15: SSK, K2tog.

Row 16: Sl st, P to end.

Row 17: SSK, fasten off, leaving 18" tail for attaching to tomato.

Attach leaves to tomato (3 leaves on front, 2 on the back) using a basting stitch along sides and edge of leaves. Weave in all ends.

Joining Tomato

With red and wrong sides of the two halves together, whip stitch around. Weave in ends.

Loop

With DPN and green, CO 3 sts.

Row 1: Knit across. Slide to right end of DPN.

Row 2: Pull yarn taut. Rep Row 1.

Repeat Rows 1 and 2 until loop measures approx 5". Join to make a loop. BO. Attach to Tomato as shown in photo.

PRETTY PLAID POTHOLDER

Finished Size: 8" x 8" (20.32 cm x 20.32 cm)

intermediate

Green vegetables look especially delicious when delivered with a green potholder.

SHOPPING LIST

Yarn

Medium-weight Cotton (4)
[2.5 ounces, 120 yards
(70.9 grams, 109 meters) per ball]
sage - 1 ball
ecru - 1 ball
[2 ounces, 99 yards
(56.7 grams, 90 meters) per ball]
greentones - 1 ball

Knitting Needles

Size 7 (4.5 mm) straight knitting needles (or size required for gauge)
Size 7 (4.5 mm) double-pointed knitting needles (DPN) (or size required for gauge)

Additional Supplies

Crochet Hook (Size H)
Large-eye yarn needle

GAUGE INFORMATION

12 sts = 2" (5.08 cm)

STITCH GUIDE

K1 with 3 wraps: insert right-hand needle into next stitch on left-hand needle, as if to knit, wrap yarn 3 times around tip of right-hand needle; now knit this stitch, carrying extra wraps on right-hand needle.

YB: with yarn to back of work
YF: with yarn to front of work

Note: *Throughout the pattern, slip each sl st (slip stitch) as if to purl. Dropped yarn is not cut, but carried loosely along the side of the work.*

INSTRUCTIONS

Body (make 2)

With sage, cast on 39 sts.

Row 1 (right side): Knit across.

Row 2: K3, K1 with 3 wraps, *K7, K1 with 3 wraps; rep from * to last 3 sts, K3. Drop sage, (do not cut); join ecru. **Note:** *Colors are carried loosely along side of work.*

Row 3: With ecru, K3, YB, sl 1, dropping extra wraps off needle; *K7, YB, sl 1 dropping extra wraps; rep from * to last 3 sts, K3.

Row 4: P3, YF, sl 1; *P7, YF, sl 1; rep from * to last 3 sts, P3. Drop ecru; join greentones.

Row 5: With greentones, K3, YB, sl 1; *K7, YB, sl 1; rep from * to last 3 sts, K3.

Instructions continued on page 8

Row 6: *K3, YF, sl 1; K3, K1 with wraps; rep from * to last 7 sts; K3, YF, sl 1, K3. Drop greentones; continue with ecru.

Row 7: *K3, YB, sl 1; K3, YB, sl 1 dropping extra wraps; rep from * to last 7 sts, K3, YB, sl 1, K3.

Row 8: P3; *YF, sl 1, P3; rep from * across. Drop ecru; continue with sage.

Row 9: K7; *YB, sl 1, K7; rep from * across.

Row 10: *K3, K1 with 3 wraps; K3, YF, sl 1; rep from * to last 7 sts; K3, K1 with 3 wraps, K3. Drop sage; continue with ecru.

Row 11: *K3, YB, sl 1 dropping extra wraps, K3, YB, sl 1; rep from * to last 7 sts; K3, YB, sl 1 dropping extra wraps, K3.

Row 12: P3; *YF, sl 1, P3; rep from * across. Drop ecru; continue with greentones.

Repeat last 8 rows (Rows 5 to 12) 5 more times. Then work the following finishing 7 rows:

Row 1: With greentones, K3, YB, sl 1; *K7, YB, sl 1; rep from * to last 3 sts, K3.

Row 2: K3, YF, sl 1; *K7, YF, sl 1; rep from * to last 3 sts, K3. Cut greentones, leaving approx. 4" end for weaving in later; continue with ecru.

Row 3: K3, YB, sl 1; *K7, YB, sl 1; rep from * to last 3 sts, K3.

Row 4: P3, YF, sl 1; *P7, YF, sl 1; rep from * to last 3 sts, P3. Cut ecru, leaving a 4" end; continue with sage.

Rows 5, 6, and 7: Knit across. BO all sts and weave in all ends.

Edging

Hold pieces with wrong sides together and BO edge of each piece at top. With sage and crochet hook, sl st into upper right-hand corner. Working through corresponding stitches of each piece, work sc evenly spaced (approx. 3 sc every 4 sts and 2 sc every other row) around all 4 sides. Work 3 sc in each corner. Finish off, leaving approximately 10" of sage yarn to be used for the loop.

Loop

With DPN and using the length of yarn attached, pick up 2 sts in the crochet edging. *K2, do not turn. Slide the stitches to the other end of the DPN*. Repeat from * to * until loop measures approx. 3". BO. Attach the loose end of the loop to the potholder.

CORN ON THE COB PAN HOLDER

Finished Size: 2½" x 6½" (6.35 cm x 16.51 cm)

Intermediate

Designed by Patricia Honaker

Grab the pan handle with this clever pan holder that mimics a corn cob.

Instructions continued on page 10

SHOPPING LIST

Yarn

Medium-weight Cotton (4)
[2.5 ounces, 120 yards
(70.9 grams, 109 meters) per ball]
yellow – 1 ball
green – 1 ball

Knitting Needles

Size 5 (3.75 mm) straight knitting needles (or size required for gauge)
Size 5 (3.75 mm) double-pointed knitting needles (DPN) (or size required for gauge)

Additional Supplies

Large-eye yarn needle

GAUGE INFORMATION

12 sts = 2" (5.08 cm)

STITCH GUIDE

BB (Bobble): [knit into front and back of stitch] twice, turn, P4, turn, K4, sl 2nd st over first st three times.

SSK (slip, slip, knit): Slip 2 sts as to knit, one at a time to right-hand needle. Insert tip of left-hand needle into fronts of these slipped sts from left to right. Knit them together: one stitch has been decreased.

M1 (Make 1): Increase one stitch by picking up the horizontal strand lying before the next stitch and knitting into the lp.

INSTRUCTIONS

With yellow, CO 24 sts.

Row 1 (wrong side): *K1, P1; rep from * across.

Row 2: *P1, K1; rep from * across.

Row 3: Repeat Row 1.

Row 4: Purl across.

Row 5: K1, *BB, K2, rep from * to last 2 sts, BB, K1.

Row 6: Knit across.

Row 7: Purl across.

Row 8: Knit across.

Repeat Rows 5 through 8 until piece measures 6" from start.

Next Row: K2tog across row: 12 sts.

Next Row: Purl.

Next Row: BO all sts, leaving a tail long enough to sew seam.
Sew the back seam.

Loop

With DPN and green, CO 3 sts.

Row 1: Knit across. Slide to right end of DPN.

Row 2: Pull yarn taut. Rep Row 1.

Repeat Rows 1 and 2 until loop measures approx 3". BO. Join to make a loop. Attach to Pan Holder as shown in photo.

Place seam of corn to the back, attach loop on either side of BO opening at top of cob.

Leaves (make 3)

With green, CO 3 sts.

Row 1 (wrong side): K1, purl across.

Row 2: K1, M1, K1, M1, K1: 5 sts

Row 3: K1, Purl across.

Row 4: K2, M1, K1, M1, K2: 7 sts.

Work evenly in stockinette stitch (knit the knit rows and purl the purl rows) until the leaf measures 2" from the cast-on edge, ending with a knit row.

Decrease Rows

Row 1: Purl across.

Row 2: SSK, knit across to last 2 sts, K2tog: 5 sts.

Repeat Rows 1 and 2: 3 sts.

Next Row: Purl across.

Last Row: SSK, K1, pass SSK over knit st to bind off.

Sew 2 leaves to the front just below the loop on the cob, tacking the tip of the leaf to the cob. Repeat the same technique with the remaining leaf on the back of the cob.

TWIN POTHOLDERS

Finished Size: 7" x 7" (17.78 cm x 17.78 cm)

EASY

These two potholders are made by a process called double knitting, which produces a piece that is the same on both sides. The stitch is used to create a double thickness for a flat piece for which extra insulation is required, such as these potholders.

SHOPPING LIST

Yarn

Medium-weight Cotton (4)
[2.5 ounces, 120 yards
(70.9 grams, 109 meters) per ball]
red - 1 ball
green - 1 ball

Knitting Needles

Size 7 (4.5 mm) straight knitting needles (or size required for gauge)
Size 7 (4.5 mm) double-pointed knitted needles (DPN) (or size required for gauge)

Additional Supplies

Large-eye yarn needle

GAUGE INFORMATION

12 sts = 2" (5.08 cm)

STITCH GUIDE

YB: with yarn to back of work
YF: with yarn to front of work

Note: *Throughout the pattern, slip each sl st (slip stitch) as if to purl. Dropped stitch is not cut, but carried loosely along the front or back of the work.*

INSTRUCTIONS

Make one of each color.
CO 44 stitches.

Rows 1 and 2: *K1; YF, sl 1, P1, sl 1; YB; rep from * across row.

Rows 3 and 4: *P1, sl 1, YB, K1, YF, sl 1; rep from * across row.

Repeat Rows 1 through 4 until the potholder measures approx. 7" (17.78 cm).
BO, working 2 sts together as one as you BO until 2 sts remain on the needle, and work loop.

Loop

Place sts on one DPN.

Row 1: With another DPN, K2; do not turn. Slide sts to opposite end of the needle.

Row 2: Take yarn around the back side of sts and with 2nd needle, K2; do not turn. Slide sts to opposite end of needle.

Rep Rows 1 and 2 until loop measures approx. 3". BO. Join cord to make loop. Weave in ends. Attach to potholder as shown in photo.

BIG APPLE POTHOLDER

Finished Size: 9½" diameter (24.13 cm)

EASY

Designed by Patricia Honaker

Serving apple pie? Much more appetizing when the pie is delivered surrounded by a big apple potholder.

SHOPPING LIST

Yarn

Medium-weight Cotton (4)
[2.5 ounces, 120 yards
(70.9 grams, 109 meters) per ball]
red – 1 ball
white – 1 ball
green – 1 ball
yellow – 1 ball

Knitting Needles

24" (60.96 cm) size 7 (4.5 mm) circular needle (or size required for gauge)
Size 7 (4.5 mm) double-pointed needles (DPN) (or size required for gauge)

Additional Supplies

Stitch markers
Large-eye yarn needle

GAUGE INFORMATION

8 sts = 2" (5.08 cm)

STITCH GUIDE

Kfb: Knit 1 in front and back of same stitch

SSK (slip, slip, knit): Slip 2 sts as to knit, one at a time to right-hand needle. Insert tip of left-hand needle into fronts of these slipped sts from left to right. Knit them together: one stitch has been decreased.

M1 (Make 1): Increase one stitch by picking up the horizontal strand lying before the next stitch and knitting into the lp.

Note: *Except for the introduction in Rows 1-5, the entire potholder is worked in rounds (Rnd). Begin the project with the double-point needles and switch to the circular needle when the number of stitches increases.*

INSTRUCTIONS

Body (make 2)

With yellow and DPN, CO 1.

Row 1: (K1, P1, K1) in same st: 3 sts.

Row 2: Purl across.

Row 3: Kfb all sts: 6 sts.

Row 4: Purl across.

Row 5: Repeat Row 3: 12 sts.

Rnd 1: Divide stitches onto 3 DPN (4 sts on each needle). Knit all sts, joining the round. Place marker on first stitch of round.

Rnd 2: *Kfb, K1; rep from * around: 18 sts.

Instructions continued on page 16

Rnd 3: Knit around.

Rnd 4: *Kfb, K1; rep from * around: 27 sts.

Rnd 5: Knit around.

Rnd 6: *Kfb, K2; rep from * around: 36 sts.

Rnd 7: Purl around; fasten off yellow.

Rnd 8: With white, *Kfb, K3; rep from * around: 45 sts.

Rnd 9: Knit around.

Rnd 10: *Kfb, K4; rep from * around: 54 sts.

Rnd 11: Knit around.

Rnd 12: *Kfb, K5; rep from * around: 63 sts.

Rnd 13: Knit around.

Rnd 14: *Kfb, K6; rep from * around: 72 sts.

Rnd 15: Knit around.

Rnd 16: *Kfb, K7; rep from * around: 81 sts.

Rnd 17: Knit around.

Rnd 18: *Kfb, K8; rep from * around: 90 sts.

Rnd 19: Knit around.

Rnd 20: *Kfb, K9; rep from * around: 99 sts.

Rnd 21: Knit around.

Rnd 22: *Kfb, K10; rep from * around: 108 sts.

Rnd 23: Knit around.

Rnd 24: *Kfb, K11; rep from * around; fasten off white: 117 sts.

Rnd 25: With red, knit around.

Rnd 26: *Kfb, K12; rep from * around: 126 sts.

Rnd 27: Purl around.

Rnd 28: *Kfb, K13; rep from * around: 135 sts.

Rnd 29: Purl around.

Rnd 30: SSK, K13, (Kfb, K14) 3 times, K15, (Kfb, K14) 3 times, Kfb, K12, K2tog, turn: 140 sts.

Rnd 31: SSK, knit to last 2 sts, K2tog, turn: 138 sts.

Rnd 32: SSK, K11, (Kfb, K15) 3 times, K15, (Kfb, K15) 3 times, Kfb, K11, K2tog, turn: 143 sts.

Rnd 33: SSK, knit to last 2 sts, K2tog: 141 sts. Bind off.

Leaf (Make 1)

With green and size 7 DPNs or straight needles, CO 3 sts.

Row 1: K1, YO, K1, YO, K1: 5 sts.

Row 2 and all even rows: Purl across.

Row 3: K2, M1, K1 M1, K2: 7 sts.

Row 5: K3, M1, K1, M1, K3: 9 sts.

Row 7: K4, M1, K1, M1, K4: 11sts.

Row 9: K5, M1,K1,M1 K5: 13 sts.

Row 11: KK6, M1, K1, M1, K6: 15 sts.

Row 13: K7, M1, K1, M1, K7: 17 sts.

Row 15: K8, M1, K1, M1, K8: 19 sts.

Row 17: SSK, K15, K2tog: 17 sts.

Row 19: SSK, K13, K2tog: 15 sts.

Row 21: SSK, K11, K2tog: 13 sts.

Row 23: SSK, K9, K2tog: 11 sts.

Row 25: SSK, K7, K2tog: 9 sts.

Row 27: SSK, K5, K2tog: 7 sts.

Row 29: SSK, K3, K2tog: 5 sts.

Row 31: SSK, K1, K2tog: 3 sts.

Row 33: SSK, slip st to left needle. K2tog.

Fasten off, leaving 12" tail for attaching to Apple. Attach to front of Apple as shown. Weave in ends.

Joining Apple

With red and wrong sides of the two halves together, whip stitch around. Weave in ends.

Loop

With DPN and green, CO 3 sts.

Row 1: Knit across. Slide to right end of needle.

Row 2: Pull yarn taut. Rep Row 1.

Repeat Rows 1 and 2 until loop measures approx 5". BO. Make a 1½" loop in end of cord and attach to Apple as shown.

WARM AND COZY POTHOLDER

Finished Size: 8" x 8" (20.32 cm x 20.32 cm)

EASY

When you bring those cookies to the dinner table, everyone will be delighted when they see the delightful colors of the potholder holding the warm platter.

SHOPPING LIST

Yarn

Medium-weight Cotton
[2 ounces, 95 yards (56.7 grams, 86 meters) per ball]
white – 1 ball
red – 1 ball

Knitting Needles

Size 7 (4.5 mm) straight knitting needles (or size required for gauge)

Additional Supplies

Crochet hook (Size H)
Large-eyed yarn needle

GAUGE INFORMATION

10 sts = 2" (5.08 cm)

STITCH GUIDE

YB: with yarn to back of work
YF: with yarn to front of work

Note: *Throughout the pattern, slip each sl st (slip stitch) as if to purl. Dropped yarn is not cut, but carried loosely along the front or back of the work.*

INSTRUCTIONS

With red, CO 35 sts.

Body (make 2)

Row 1 (right side): Knit across.

Row 2: K1; *P3, K3; rep from * to last 4 sts; P3, K1. Drop red (do not cut; continue with white).

Row 3: With white, K1, YB (with yarn to back of work) sl 3; *K3, YB sl 3; rep from * to last st, K1.

Row 4: K1, P1, YF (with yarn to front of work) sl 1; *P5, YF sl 1; rep from * to last 2 sts P1, K1.

Row 5: Knit across with white.

Row 6: K4; *P3, K3; rep from * to last st, K1. Drop white; continue with red.

Row 7: With red, K4; *YB, sl 3, K3; rep from * to last st, K1.

Row 8: K1, P4; *YF, sl 1, P5; rep from * to last 6 sts; YF, sl 1, P4, K1.

Rep Rows 1 through 8, 6 times more; then rep Rows 1 and 2 once. BO all sts evenly across.

Edging

Hold both pieces with wrong sides together and BO edge of each piece at top. Working through corresponding sts of each piece with crochet hook and red yarn, sl st at upper right-hand corner; work in sc evenly spaced (approx. 3 sc every 4 sts and 2 sc every other row) around all 4 sides, and work 3 sc at each corner. Finish off, leaving approx. 10" of red yarn to be used for loop.

Loop

With crochet hook, ch 20. Turn. Sc in 2nd chain from hook and in each rem chain. Finish off. Attach loose end to the pot holder to make a loop.

WORLD'S QUICKEST DISHCLOTH

Finished Size: 7" x 7" (17.78 cm x 17.78 cm)

EASY

Make it in a snap; use it forever.

SHOPPING LIST

Yarn

Medium-weight Cotton (4)
[2.5 ounces, 120 yards (70.9 grams, 109 meters)per ball]
ecru –1 ball

Knitting Needles

Size 7 (4.5 mm) straight knitting needles (or size required for gauge)

GAUGE INFORMATION

8 sts = 2" (in garter stitch, knit each row)

INSTRUCTIONS

CO 2 sts.

Row 1: Knit across

Row 2: K1, YO, K1: 3 sts.

Note: *Throughout pattern, each YO counts as one stitch.*

Row 3: Knit across.

Row 4: K1, (YO, K1) twice: 5 sts.

Row 5: Knit across.

Row 6: K1, YO, knit to last st, YO, K1: 7 sts.

Row 7: Knit.

Repeat Rows 6 and 7 until 43 sts are on needle.

DECREASING

Row 1: K1, YO, K2tog; knit to last 3 sts, K2tog, YO, K1.

Row 2: K2, K2tog; knit to last 4 sts, K2tog, K2.

Repeat last 2 rows until 9 sts remain on needle. Continue decreasing as follows:

Row 1: K1, YO; (K2tog) twice, K1; K2tog, YO, K1: 8 sts.

Row 2: K2, (K2tog) twice, K2: 6 sts.

Row 3: K1, YO; (K2tog) twice, YO, K1: 6 sts.

Row 4: K1, (K2tog) twice, K1: 4 sts.

Row 5: (K2tog) twice: 2 sts.

Row 6: K2tog.

Finish off; weave in all ends.

DISHCLOTH IN THE ROUND

Finished Size: 8½" (21.59 cm)

EASY

As you wash around and around, all the dishes come clean.

SHOPPING LIST

Yarn

Medium-weight Cotton
[3 ounces, 150 yards (85 grams, 138 meters) per ball]
blue multi color – 1 ball

Knitting Needles

24" (60.96 cm) size 7 (4.5 mm) circular knitting needle (or size required for gauge)
Size 7 (4.5mm) double point needles (DPN) (or size required for gauge)

Additional Supplies

Small safety pin or stitch marker

GAUGE INFORMATION

20 sts = 4" (10.16 cm) in stock st (knit 1 row, purl 1 row)

STITCH GUIDE

M5 (Make 5): (K1, P1) twice, K1 all in same stitch.

INSTRUCTIONS

Note: *Mark beg of rnds with stitch marker or small safety pin.*

Note: *Begin project with DPN and switch to circular needle when the number of stitches increases.*

CO 9 sts onto one DPN. Divide the sts evenly onto 3 needles; join, being careful not to twist sts.

Rnd 1: Knit.

Rnd 2: Knit and purl into each stitch: 18 sts.

Rnd 3: *K1, P1; rep from * around.

Rnd 4: *P1, K1; rep from * around.

Rnd 5: Rep Rnd 3.

Rnd 6: Rep Rnd 2: 36 sts.

Rnds 7 through 12: Rep Rnds 3 and 4.

Rnd 13: Rep Rnd 2: 72 sts.

Rnds 14 through 19: Rep Rnds 3 and 4.

Rnd 20: Rep Rnd 2: 144 sts.

Rnd 21: Rep Rnd 4.

Rnd 22: Rep Rnd 3.

Rnd 23: Rep Rnd 4.

Rnd 24: Rep Rnd 2: 288 sts.

Rnd 25: Rep Rnd 4.

Rnd 26: *K2tog, YO, K2tog, turn; P1, M5, P1, sl 1 as if to purl, turn, BO 7 sts (one st remains on right needle); rep from * around.

Finish off; weave in yarn ends.

FISHY DISHCLOTH

Finished Size: 9" (22.86 cm)

EASY

Designed by Michelle Wilcox for Red Heart®

Use a fish to wash a dish, or at least a dishcloth that looks like a fish.

SHOPPING LIST

Yarn

Medium-weight Polyester (4)
[3.5 ounces, 92 yards,
(100 grams, 85 meters) per skein]
green – 1 skein
blue – 1 skein

Knitting Needles

Size 7 (4.5 mm) straight knitting needles (or size required for gauge)

Additional Supplies

Large-eye yarn needle
Small amount black yarn

GAUGE INFORMATION

Gauge is not required nor critical for this project.

STITCH GUIDE

Kfb: Knit 1 in front and back of same stitch.

INSTRUCTIONS

Make one of each color.

Beginning at mouth, CO 6 sts.

Rows 1 through 3: Knit across.

Row 4: K2tog, K2, K2tog: 4 sts.

Row 5: Knit across.

Row 6: K1, (Kfb) twice, K1: 6 sts.

Row 7: K1, Kfb, knit to last 2 sts, Kfb, K1: 8 sts.

Rows 8-12: Repeat Row 7: 18 sts after working Row 12.

Row 13: Knit across.

Rows 14-17: Repeat Row 7: 26 sts after working Row 17.

Row 18: Knit.

Rows 19-20: Repeat Row 7: 30 sts after working last row.

Knit every row until piece measures 4" (10.16 cm) from beginning.

Instructions continued on page 26

Shaping Bottom Fin

Row 1 (Next Row): Cast on 5 sts to piece. Knit all sts to end of row: 35 sts.

Row 2: Knit across.

Row 3: Bind off 5 sts. Knit to end of row: 30 sts.

Knit every row until piece now measures 5" (12.7 cm) from beginning of entire project, ending with Bottom Fin at end of row.

Shaping Top Fin

Row 1 (Next Row): Cast on 5 sts to piece. Knit all sts to end of row: 35 sts.

Rows 2-6: Knit across.

Row 7: K2tog, knit to end of row: 34 sts.

Row 8: Knit across.

Row 9: K2tog, knit to end of row: 33 sts.

Row 10: Knit across.

Row 11: K2tog, knit to end of row: 32 sts.

Row 12: Knit across.

Row 13: Bind off 2 sts. Knit to end of row: 30 sts.

Row 14: K1, K2tog, knit to last 3 sts, K2tog, K1: 28 sts.

Repeat Row 14 eight more times: 12 sts on last row worked.

Shaping Tail

Row 1 (Next Row): Kfb in each st across piece: 24 sts.

Knit every row until Tail measures 2" (5.08 cm)

Bind off entire piece.

SIDE FIN (make 2)

Cast on 10 sts.

Rows 1-4: Knit across.

Row 5: K2tog, knit to last 2 sts, K2tog: 8 sts.

Row 6: Knit across.

Row 7: Repeat Row 5: 6 sts.

Row 8: Knit across.

Row 9: Repeat Row 5: 4 sts.

Bind off.

FINISHING

Sew Side Fins in center of either side of Fish. Weave in all ends.

With black yarn, embroider an eye on each side in satin st.

SWIRLING DISHCLOTH

Finished Size: 8" (20.32 cm)

EASY

As you swirl around and around with this dishcloth, all the dishes are certain to come out clean.

Instructions continued on page 28

SHOPPING LIST

Yarn

Medium-weight Cotton (4)
[2.5 ounces, 120 yards
(70.9 grams, 109 meters) per ball]
purple – 1 ball
[3 ounces, 150 yards (85
grams, 138 meters) per ball]
multl-color – 1 ball

Knitting Needles

Size 7 (4.5 mm) straight knitting needles (or size required for gauge)

Additional Supplies

Large-eye yarn needle

GAUGE INFORMATION

8 sts = 2" (5.08 cm) in garter st (knit every row)

INSTRUCTIONS

With multi-color, CO 15 sts.

Rows 1, 3, 5 and 7: Knit 15.

Row 2: K3, YO, K11; turn, leaving 1 st on needle.

Row 4: K3, YO, K11; turn, leaving 2 sts on needle.

Row 6: K3, YO, K11; turn, leaving 3 sts on needle.

Row 8: Bind off 3 sts; K2, YO, K8; turn, leaving 4 sts on needle.

Rows 9, 11 and 13: Knit 12.

Row 10: K3, YO, K8; turn, leaving 5 sts on needle.

Row 12: K3, YO, K8; turn, leaving 6 sts on needle.

Row 14: Bind off 3 sts; K2, YO, K5; turn, leaving 7 sts on needle.

Rows 15, 17 and 19: Knit 9.

Row 16: K3, YO, K5; turn, leaving 8 sts on needle.

Row 18: K3, YO, K5; turn, leaving 9 sts on needle.

Row 20: Bind off 3 sts; knit remaining 14 sts.

Rows 21 through 40: With purple, rep Rows 1 through 20.

Rows 41 through 60: With multi-color, rep Rows 1 through 20.

Rows 61 through 80: With purple, rep Rows 1 through 20.

Rows 81 through 100: With multi-color, rep Rows 1 through 20.

Rows 101 through 120: With purple, rep Rows 1 through 20.

Rows 121 through 140: With multi-color, rep Rows 1 through 20.

Rows 141 through 160: With purple, rep Rows 1 through 20.

Bind off, leaving an 18" end.

Carefully matching sts, sew cast-on edge to BO edge, forming a swirled circle.

General Information

ABBREVIATIONS

BB	bobble	rem	remain(ing)
BO	bind off	rep	repeat
cm	centimeter	rnd(s)	round(s)
CO	cast on	sc	single crochet
DPN	double-pointed knitting needles	sl	slip
		sl st(s)	slip stitch(es)
K	knit	SSK	slip, slip, knit
Kfb	knit in front and back of same stitch	st(s)	stitch(es)
		tog	together
K2tog	knit two stitches together	YB	yarn in back of needle
M1	increase one stitch	YF	yarn in front of needle
mm	millimeter(s)		
P	purl	YO	yarn over needle

KNIT AND CROCHET TERMINOLOGY

The patterns in this book have been written using the knitting and crochet terminology that is used in the United States. Terms which may have different equivalents in other parts of the world are listed below:

United States	**International**
Gauge	Tension
Skip	Miss
Yarn over (YO)	Yarn forward (yfwd) or yarn around needle (yrn)
Bind off	Cast off
Slip stitch	Single crochet
Single crochet	Double crochet
Double crochet	Treble crochet

GAUGE

Gauge simply means the number of stitches per inch that results from a specified yarn worked with needles in a specified size. But since everyone knits—some loosely, some tightly, some in-between—the measurements of individual work can very greatly. Before beginning a project, therefore, make a sample swatch in the yarn and needle specified in the individual instructions. After the swatch has been completed, measure it, counting the stitches and rows carefully. If the swatch is larger or smaller than specified, make another swatch, changing the needle size to get the gauge.

Yarn manufacturers, publishers, needle and hook manufacturers have worked together to set up a series of guidelines and symbols to bring uniformity to patterns. Before beginning a project, check to see if your skill level is equal to the one listed for the project.

Beginner	Projects for first-time knitters using basic knit and purl stitches. Minimal shaping.
Easy	Projects using basic stitches, repetitive stitch patterns, simple color changes, and simple shaping and finishing.
Intermediate	Projects using a variety of stitches, such as basic cables and lace, simple intarsia, double-pointed needles and knitting in the round needle techniques, mid-level shaping and finishing.
Experienced	Projects using advanced techniques and stitches, such as short rows, fair isle, more intricate intarsia, cables, lace patterns, and numerous color changes.

To make it easier for yarn manufacturers, publishers, and designers to prepare consumer-friendly products and for consumers to select the right materials for a project, the following standard yarn weight system has been adopted.

Standard Yarn Weight System
Categories of yarn, gauge, ranges, and recommended needle and hook sizes

Yarn Weight Symbol & Category	0 Lace	1 Super Fine	2 Fine	3 Light	4 Medium	5 Bulky	6 Super Bulky	7 Jumbo
Type of Yarns in Category	Fingering 10 count crochet thread	Sock Fingering, Baby	Sport, Baby	DK, Light, Worsted	Worsted, Afghan, Aran	Chunky, Craft, Rug	Bulky, Roving	Jumbo, Roving
Knit Gauge Range* in Stockinette St itchto 4 inches	33-40** sts	27-32 sts	23-26 sts	21-24 sts	16-20 sts	12-15 sts	7-11 sts	6 sts and fewer
Recommended Needle in Metric Size Range	1.5-2.25mm	2.25-3.25mm	3.25-3.75mm	3.75-4.5mm	4.5-5.5mm	5.5-8mm	8-12.75mm	12.75mm and larger
Recommended Needle US Size Range	000 to 1	1 to 3	3 to 5	5 to 7	7 to 9	9 to 11	11 to 17	17 and larger

* **GUIDELINES ONLY:** The above reflect the most commonly used gauges and needle sizes for specific yarn categories.

** Lace weight yarns are usually knitted on larger needles to create lacy, openwork patterns. Accordingly, a gauge range is difficult to determine. Always follow the gauge stated in your pattern.

YARN INFORMATION

Potholders and dishcloths in this book were made using a variety of yarns. Any brand of the specified weight of yarn may be used. It is best to refer to yardage/meters when determining how many balls to purchase.

For your convenience, listed below are the specific yarns used to create our photography models. Because yarn manufacturers make frequent changes in the their product lines, you may sometimes find it necessary to use a substitute yarn or to search for the discontinued product at alternate suppliers (locally or online).

TOMATO POTHOLDER
Lily® Cotton Sugar 'n Cream®
#95 Red
#84 Sage Green

PRETTY PLAID POTHOLDER
Lily® Cotton Sugar 'n Cream®
#84 Sage Green
#04 Soft Ecru
Red Heart ®Crème de la Crème™
#149 Greentones

CORN ON THE COB PAN HOLDER
Lily® Cotton Sugar 'n Cream®
#84 Sage Green
#73 Sunshine

TWIN POTHOLDERS
Lily® Cotton Sugar 'n Cream®
#95 Red
#11 Forest Green

BIG APPLE POTHOLDER
Lily® Cotton Sugar 'n Cream®
#95 Red
#1 White
#84 Sage Green
#73 Yellow

WARM AND COZY POTHOLDER
Lily® Cotton Sugar 'n Cream®
#95 Red
#1 White

WORLD'S QUICKEST DISHCLOTH
Lily® Cotton Sugar 'n Cream®
#4 Soft Ecru

DISHCLOTH IN THE ROUND
Lily® Cotton Sugar 'n Cream®
#07 Swimming Pool

FISHY DISHCLOTH
Red Heart® Scrubby™
#620 Lime
#501 Ocean

SWIRLING DISHCLOTH
Lily® Cotton Sugar 'n Cream®
#1318 Black Currant
#2135 Moondance

Production Team: Pattern Testers: Kimberly Britt and Patricia Honaker; Technical Editor: Mary Ann Frits; Book Design: Linda Causee

Produced for Leisure Arts by Creative Partners™LLC